Nuggets of Encouragement

Receiving God's Blessing Through
Our Christian Walk

Dr. Rebekah McCloud

Nuggets of Encouragement: Receiving God's Blessing Through
Our Christian Walk
by Dr. Rebekah McCloud

Cover and Interior Design by Big Easy Creative
Front Cover Image licensed for use from Adobe.com

Order Direct
https://www.drrebekahmccloud.com

ISBN 978-0-9748179-5-8

Produced and Printed in the United States of America
10 9 8 7 6 5 4 3 2

The views expressed in this work are solely of the author
and do not necessarily reflect the views of the publisher,
who hereby disclaims any responsibility for them.

Copyright © 2024 Dr. Rebekah McCloud. All rights reserved.

No part of this book may be used or reproduced by any means,
graphic, electronic, or mechanical, including photocopying, recording,
taping, or by any information storage retrieval system without the
written permission of the publisher except in the case of brief
quotations embodied in critical articles and reviews.

Nuggets of Encouragement

Receiving God's Blessing Through
Our Christian Walk

Dr. Rebekah McCloud

Dedication

This book is dedicated to my parents, Rev. Arcollo McCloud, Sr., and Mrs. Ilean McCloud, who read and studied the Bible daily. They provided me with a firm Christian foundation and a strong work ethic. I still hold to these today. They anchored me and defined who I am and to whom I belong.

Acknowledgments

Thank you to Missionary Alice Jackson Gordon for serving as my proofreader. My dear sister in Christ, I appreciate your encouragement, eagle eyes, friendship, and time.

Thank you to Minister Charles Barfield, Esq. for the opportunity to start writing these nuggets. I appreciate your confidence in me and your constant encouragement.

Thank you to Pastor Tedd Washington (posthumously); he saw this book before I did. I appreciate his nudges and prayers.

Thank you to my family, friends, and the Grace for Living Ministries family. I appreciate your kind words, well wishes, prayers, and encouragement.

Thank you to my aunt, Jessie Brundidge, for always sharing the word of God with me. Her devotion and belief have been a light to my path.

Thank you to my grandson, Kevin Sharpe, Jr. His antics, curiosity, and weekly questions were the impetus for many nuggets.

May God continue to bless all of you.

Note from the Author

The themes of this journal are blessings and our daily walk. The pages of the Bible are filled with stories regarding the many blessings God has in store for us (Psalm 34:8), the way to receive a blessing (Psalm 1:1-3), and God's encouragement to us to be a blessing to others (Proverbs 22:9 & Luke 6:38). God's blessings have healed the sick (Matthew 9: 20-21), raised the dead (John 11:38-44), given salvation (Luke 23: 42-43), won battles (2 Chronicles 20:15), and extended territories (1 Chronicles 4:10). Be assured, God is still in the blessing business. His well never runs dry. Our daily walk was beautifully outlined by Paul in Colossians 1 (verses 9-14). Being a child of God means that we follow in the footsteps of our Lord and Savior. At times we walk side by side with the Lord, at other times he carries us; but know, he has already gone ahead to pave the way (Deuteronomy 31:8). In this walk, we have "been born again, not of perishable seed, but of imperishable, through the living and enduring word of God," (1 Peter 1:23).

This journal allows readers to consider their everyday lives from a fresh perspective. The real-life stories are anchored with scriptures to illustrate a point and for further studies. Each entry poses four questions for consideration. What are my key takeaways from this teaching is the first question. It allows readers to enumerate points that piqued their interest, resonated with them, or led them to study. The takeaways are different for each reader. Questions two and three are specific to each entry. There are no right or wrong answers. The questions provide readers with a vehicle by which they will give honest reflections. These questions are not a diagnostic or counseling tool. Accept them as food for thought. Question number four asks what are my next steps. It allows the reader to seek insight and God's direction in moving forward. The journal also includes opportunities for readers to recap and apply their learning.

Walking with God means we have a relationship with him. Our connection is personal, present, and unique to each of us. Our walk allows for conversation, fellowship, examination, and learning. It requires that we are born again (John 3:3), transformed (Romans 12:2), and are worthy of God's calling (Ephesians 4:1-6). As you move through this journal, reflect on your walk with the Lord. His spirit dwells in us (1 Corinthians 3:16). May this journal be a tool that enhances and strengthens your walk with God.

—Dr. Rebekah

Table of Contents

Armor Up	13
Be Vigilant	19
Dial G-O-D	25
Call on the Lord	29
We Have a Situation	35
I Surrender All	41
Plop, Plop, Fizz, Fizz	45
Do you Believe?	49
Recap & Apply	53
The B Word	57
Chosen: So Do Not Look Back	63
Upstaged	69
What's Your Theme Song?	75
Can We Talk	79
High Expectations	85
Blind, but Now I See	91
Keep Your Mouth	97
Recap & Apply	101
Change my Name	105
Ought To	111

Is God Your Co-pilot?	115
Do You Hear Him?	119
S.A.V.I.O.R.	125
Work to Do	131
Close Enough for a Blessing	137
What are you Waiting For?	141
Recap & Apply	147

Armor Up

It seems like every time you hear or see the news, it is filled with murder, mayhem, and madness. My momma would say, "People are doing anything they are big enough to do. God sees them." Is this a sign of the times? Are things unfolding as the Bible predicts? Perhaps. 2 Timothy 3: 1-5 tells us, "But understand this, that in the last days there will come times of difficulty. For people will be lovers of self, lovers of money, proud, arrogant, abusive, disobedient to their parents, ungrateful, unholy, heartless, unappeasable, slanderous, without self-control, brutal, not loving good, treacherous, reckless, swollen with conceit, lovers of pleasure rather than lovers of God, having the appearance of godliness, but denying its power. Avoid such people." Matthew 24:12 says, "Because of the increase of wickedness, the love of most will grow cold."

We are indeed living in difficult times. It is depressing, depleting, and debilitating. It makes me want to holler and throw up both of my hands. But is this what God has called His people to do? I think not. God is asking His people to come into partnership with Him.

Remember, we are always a part of the problem or a part of the solution. God wants a willing people, some warriors who will be watchful, available, and will not fall asleep on Him. I want to be part of the solution.

We need to prepare for battle. Ephesians 6: 10-17 says, "Finally, my brethren, be strong in the Lord, and in the power of his might. Put on the whole armor of God, that ye may be able to stand against the wiles of the devil. For we wrestle not against flesh and blood, but against principalities, against powers, against the rulers of the darkness of this world, against spiritual wickedness in high places. Wherefore take unto you the whole armor of God, that ye may be able to withstand in the evil day, and having done all, to stand. Stand therefore, having your loins girth about with truth, and having on the breastplate of righteousness; And your feet shod with the preparation of the gospel of peace; Above all, taking the shield of faith, wherewith ye shall be able to quench all the fiery darts of the wicked. And take the helmet of salvation, and the sword of the Spirit, which is the word of God."

Will we be perfect at it? No, none is perfect but God. But we cannot let that stop us. We must keep going; keep trying. A colleague said it best. "My steadfast prayer is for Him to use me according to His good purpose, strengthen me, and help me be His light in the world - be it at home, work, grocery store, church, wherever. Some days are better than others but He's steadfast working on me. I am the common denominator in each lesson He takes me through. God gives us repeats until we get it right!"

Consider that for a minute. "God gives us repeats until we get it right!" He is our rock, our fortress, and our strong tower. With Him, we will not be shaken; we will not be moved. Isaiah 40:31 says, that the Lord will renew our strength, we will mount up with wings like eagles, we will run and not be weary, we will walk and not faint. Take heart, all. God has got this. We are the common denominator. We can be His light. We can make a difference. Let us armor up and get to work!

Prayer

Lord, thank you for your armor and your protection. The battle is a part of life and is ahead of me. With your help, I know I will be victorious. Amen.

Reflection

What are my key takeaways from this teaching?

Am I prepared for the battle?

Who or what is my biggest adversary?

What are my next steps?

Be Vigilant

Recently, the police sent out an alert titled "Be Vigilant About Your Safety." The alert was designed to remind people to protect themselves from scammers and thieves. The alert included three reminders that we can use to strengthen our Christian walk.

First, it said, "use smart judgment." There are over 100 scriptures in the Bible about judgment. But, Proverbs 3 is my "go-to." Verse 13 says, "Happy is the man that finds wisdom and gets understanding." And verse 21 tells us not to "lose sight of these—keep sound wisdom and discretion." We are living in a time when I wonder if people use any judgment. You turn on the TV and people are trying to excuse their actions and use terms such as "cloudy judgment, a lapse in judgment, or an error of judgment." Regardless, these are excuses for making poor decisions and living lives contrary to God's word. Psalm 119:66 says, "I believe in your commands; now teach me good judgment and knowledge."

Second, it said, "be wary of fraud." The dictionary provides several synonyms for the word fraud. They include deceit, false, fake, counterfeit, imitation, con, scheme, and scam. The alert warned about fraud: fraudulent dealings, fraudulent acts, and fraudulent people. The Bible also warns us about fraud. There are about 50 verses that address it. Matthew 24:24 says, "False messiahs and false prophets will appear and perform great signs and wonders to deceive, if possible, the very elect." And, Matthew 7:15 says, "Watch out for false prophets. They come to you in sheep's clothing, but inwardly they are ferocious wolves." Everything that glitters is not gold. Let us be like the three wise monkeys: see no evil, hear no evil, and speak no evil. We must guard our eyes, our ears, our mouths, and our minds. Proverbs 4:23 says "Above all else, guard your heart, for everything you do flows from it." Let us be vigilant.

Third, it said to "be aware of your surroundings, vigilant of activity around you, and attentive to individuals approaching, walking purposely, and with confidence." Good advice. Let us take caution not to act like Peter. In the Garden of Gethsemane, the night before Jesus was arrested, Jesus asked Peter and two others to stay and watch with him. Matthew 26:40 says, "Then he [speaking of Jesus] returned to his disciples and found them sleeping. "Couldn't you men keep watch with me for one hour?" The critical piece of the passage is verse 41. Jesus tells them to "Watch and pray so that you will not fall into temptation. The spirit is willing, but the flesh is weak."

I can truthfully say that there are times when my spirit is oh so willing, but my flesh is more than weak; it is worn out. When I am tired, weary, and frustrated I need to be especially on guard. These are often the times when the Devil attacks. He approaches walking purposely and with confidence. He slides up, gets in my face, or whispers in my ear. The Bible says the Devil "goes around like a roaring lion" but can also "masquerade as an angel of light."

Romans 16:20 says, "The God of peace will soon crush Satan under your feet. May the grace of our Lord Jesus be with you." Be vigilant.

Prayer

Father, thank you for your covering as I am vigilant each day. Open my eyes, guard my heart, and bind the Devil. Your word is my shield and your presence is my comforter. I trust in you. Amen.

Reflection

What are my key takeaways from this teaching?

About what do I need to be more vigilant?

How can I ensure that both my spirit and my flesh are willing?

What are my next steps?

Dial G-O-D

The US has the largest Christian population in the world. About 71% of Americans identify as Christians. Over 310 million smartphone users reside in the US. There are diehard iPhone users and equally diehard Android users. Some treat their phones like an appendage and take them everywhere they go. Others use it when needed. Some subscribe to T-Mobile, AT&T, Verizon, Cricket, Metro PCS, or utilize some other service. No matter the make of our phone or service provider, they are a fact of life. Most people use them daily. Many would be lost without one. Question: what if we used God like we use our cell phones?

When we have an emergency or need help, we dial 911. That call dispatches police, fire, and emergency personnel. What if we dialed G-O-D? The Bible says in Psalm 50:15, "Call to me when trouble comes, I will save you." Psalm 145:18 says, "The Lord is near to all who call on him." Finally, Romans 10:13 assures us, "Everyone who calls on the name of the Lord shall be saved." God is our refuge and strength, a very present help in our time of trouble (Psalm 46:1).

Remember, when we dial 911 also call God. He is on the main line; call him up and tell him what you want.

When we want information or knowledge, we dial 411 and ask Google, Siri, or Alexa. Try dialing G-O-D. His information and knowledge will transform our lives. Romans 11:33 proclaims, "Oh, how great are God's riches and wisdom and knowledge!" James 1:5 says, "If any of you lacks wisdom, he should ask God, who gives generously. Proverbs 13:13-14 tells us, "Blessed are those who find wisdom, those who gain understanding for she is more profitable than silver and yields better returns than gold." Google opens a world of knowledge to us. But nothing beats God's seven gifts of knowledge: wisdom, understanding, counsel, fortitude, knowledge, piety, and the fear of God (Isaiah 11: 2-3).

When we need help navigating, we use the GPS on our phones. It gives us step-by-step directions from point A to point B. When we call on G-O-D, he will teach us the way to go (Psalm 32:8), guide us continually (Isaiah 58:11), make our paths straight (Proverbs 3:6), and direct our steps (Proverbs 6:9). The word of the Lord is a lamp for our feet and a light for our path (Psalm 32:8). Although GPS is not always 100% accurate, God is. Psalm 37:2-3 tells us, "The Lord makes firm the steps of the ones who delight in him; though he may stumble, he will not fail, for the Lord upholds him with his hand."

For most, cell phones are part of our daily use; let us not forget to use God daily. We do that through reading his word, praise and worship, gratitude, kindness, and prayer. I guarantee at the end of the month, there will not be a bill. God is free to all. The Lord stands at the door and knocks (Revelations 3:20). Open it and let him in. Utilizing G-O-D in addition to 911, 411, and GPS is just the beginning of what God has in store for us. Oh, the places we will go; eyes have not seen, nor ears heard.

Prayer

God, thank you for meeting our needs in an emergency, providing valuable information, and directing us to our destination. You, the great I Am, make all things possible. Amen.

Reflection

What are my key takeaways from this teaching?

What situation in my life needs GOD instead of 911?

On my current journey, where can I utilize GOD as my GPS?

What are my next steps?

Call on the Lord

My momma had her own language. Sometimes she used words I had never heard before. I came to appreciate the beauty of her language. She often spoke in similes and metaphors and used alliterations and idioms. She quoted scriptures and hymns, and sometimes made sounds and utterances.

One time we went to the doctor, and he asked her how she was doing. She just made a sound, "Oomph," and pumped her fist. He said, "Tell me more about that. Can you describe it?" She said I feel like a nasty rag." He chuckled and said, "Mrs. McCloud, I've never heard it said that way, but I think I know what you mean."

How often do we use grunts, groans, and gestures to communicate in hopes that others will understand? How often do we use utterances? The dictionary says an utterance is a "spoken word, statement, or vocal sound. It is the smallest unit of speech." Its size has nothing to do with its impact or its meaning. Most of us have some understanding of a situation when we hear someone utter "Oomph."

But do we understand the significance of what it means to call on, to utter, the name of God the Father, God the Son, or God the Holy Spirit? Or to call on, or utter, the name of Jesus Christ, the Lord? So many of those that we read about in the Bible, called on the Lord. Moses, David, Job, Esther, Hannah, Ruth, Paul, John, and so on called on the Lord. When my mother was in distress, she called on the name of Jesus. Do we know what it means to call on the Lord?

People use the name of the Lord so frivolously these days. OMG (Oh My God) has become a part of popular culture. Even church folk use it in their conversations, correspondences, text messages, and social media. The acronym is usually used to express an extreme reaction: surprise, alarm, or disgust. Back to my original question: Do we know what it means to call on the Lord? We should!

There is love (Psalm 86:15), peace (2 Thessalonians 3:16), hope (Psalm 33: 20-22), and restoration (1 Peter 5:10) in the name of Jesus. There is no surprise, alarm, or disgust.

- There is joy in the name of Jesus. Romans 15: 13 says, "May the God of hope fill you with all joy and peace as you trust in him, so that you may overflow with hope by the power of the Holy Spirit."
- There is salvation in the Name of Jesus! Acts 4:12 says, "Salvation is found in no one else, for there is no other name under heaven given to men by which we must be saved."
- There is healing in the Name of Jesus! James 5:14 says, "Is any one of you sick? He should call the elders of the church to pray over him and anoint him with oil in the name of the Lord."
- There is victory in the Name of Jesus! Deuteronomy 20:4 says, "For the LORD your God is the one who goes with

> you to fight for you against your enemies to give you victory."
> - There is protection in the Name of Jesus! Proverbs 18:10 says, "The name of the LORD is a strong tower; the righteous run to it and are safe."
> - There is favor in the Name of Jesus! 2 Corinthians 1:20 tells us that, "For no matter how many promises God has made, they are "Yes" in Christ. And so through him, the "Amen" is spoken by us to the glory of God."

Romans 10:13 says, "Everyone who calls on the name of the Lord will be saved." Psalm 18:6 says, "In my distress I called upon the LORD, and cried to my God for help; He heard my voice out of His temple, and my cry for help before Him came into His ears." When I was a kid, we used to sing a song that said, "Jesus on the mainline, tell him what you want; call him up and tell him what you want."

My prayer is that I know that I know what it means to call on the Lord. No OMG, no surprise, alarm, or disgust! Instead, love, peace, joy, favor, victory, healing, protection, hope, restoration, and salvation will be mine. Amen!

Prayer

Lord, thank you that I can call your name. Your name is precious and is a name above all names. You are a shield and a comforter for me. Amen.

Reflection

What are my key takeaways from this teaching?

Do I know what it means to call on the Lord?

For what do I need to call on the Lord?

What are my next steps?

We Have a Situation

There is a commercial of a young boy running to the bathroom only to get there and is unable to open his belt. He calls out, "Mom, we have a situation." How often have we found ourselves in a situation: a difficult situation, sticky situation, dangerous situation, bad, embarrassing, stressful, or crazy situation? Who do we call? Do we call out "God, we have a situation?"

God uses our situations to examine our lives. Some of us are like an egg; you must crack it to see what is inside. When we are in a situation, on close examination, what will God find in our lives? Will he find a people who focus on God instead of our situation? Will he find a people who tell our God how big our situation is, or will he find a people who tell our situation how big our God is? We serve an awesome God and should always be able to tell him "We have a situation."

After he examines our lives, God uses our situations to redirect our steps. His intervention is like a rudder on a ship. He helps us to change our ways or our paths. He lights a fire under us or gives us a wake-up call. In the end, He wants to lead us to a higher level of trust in him. Philippians 4:6-7 reminds us, "Do not be anxious about anything, but in every situation, by prayer and petition, with thanksgiving, present your requests to God. And the peace of God, which transcends all understanding, will guard your hearts and your minds in Christ Jesus." Amen.

God uses our situations to correct us. Sometimes we can be some contrary people. We know what God expects from us. He has gifted us all with at least one talent and he makes it possible for us to have all that we do (great or small). Yet, we sometimes fail to deliver. We fail to use our time, talent, money, and resources to further the kingdom. I am so glad that failure is transitory and that failure is not a person; it is an event. If we hold to God's unchanging hand, he will lead us to turn failure into success. Isaiah 42:16 says he, "will lead the blind along a path they never knew to places where they have never been before. I will change darkness into light for them. I will make the rough ground smooth. I will do these things for them; I will not abandon my people." If he does it for them, I know he will do it for me. Proverbs 3:5-6 reminds us to, "Trust in the Lord with all your heart and lean not on your own understanding; in all your ways submit to Him, and He will make your paths straight." Situations help us to build character, to build strength, and to build understanding.

Having a situation does not mean God is not with us. He is always with us and always working for our good. No matter what we call him—Jehovah Jireah, Jehovah Nissi, Jehovah Rapha, Jehovah Shalom, Elohim, El Shaddai, Comforter, Savior, King of Glory, Almighty, Bread of Life, Master, Rose of Sharon, Good Shepherd, Counselor, Deliverer, Spirit of Truth, Great High Priest, Strong Tower, Bright and Morning Star, Lamb of God, I Am that

I Am, Friend, Hiding Place, Prince of Peace, Horn of Salvation, Wheel in the middle of a wheel, Redeemer, Alpha and Omega, God the Father, God the Son, or God the Holy Ghost—no matter what we call him, let us remember to call God when we have a situation.

Prayer

God, I have a situation. I am so glad I can come to you with anything that concerns me. I thank you for your examination of my life, correction, and redirection. Amen.

Reflection

What are my key takeaways from this teaching?

What situation do I need to talk about with God?

What correction or redirection might God need to provide for me?

What are my next steps?

I Surrender All

Do you have a friend who has said, "I cannot give my time to God because I am too busy?" Or, "I got too much to do. I am overworked, overloaded, and overlooked." Tell your friend to say, "I am blessed and highly favored. The Lord is my strength and will allow me to mount up on wings like an eagle. I will run and not grow weary," (Isaiah 40:31). The Bible tells us in Ephesians 5:15 and Colossians 4:5 to make the best use of our time. How can we do that? We can surrender it all to God. We must surrender those things that keep us too busy, overworked, and worn out. It is not our time; it is his. Surrender all and watch him work.

Do you have a friend who has said, "I cannot use my talent because nobody asked me?" Or "I cannot do it like so and so does." Or "God did not give me any talent. I cannot sing, dance, or play an instrument." Tell your friend we all have talent; all of God's children have shoes! Tell your friend to make a joyful noise unto the Lord anyhow. Psalm 98:5 says, "Make a loud noise, and rejoice, and sing praises." Remember, talent is a gift from God. Proverbs 18:16 says,

"A man's gifts will make room for him." How can we make this work, you might ask? We must surrender our doubts, our fears, and those voices in our heads that tell us we are not enough. Give them to God and watch him work. It is not our talent; it is his. Surrender all!

Do you have a friend who has said, "I cannot give my treasure to God because I am broke, busted, and behind?" Or asks "What is that preacher going to do with my money; I only have a few crumbs?" Tell your friend that the treasure is not ours; it all belongs to God. Matthew 6:19 warns us, "Do not store up for yourselves treasures on earth, where moths and vermin destroy, and where thieves break in and steal." Instead, we should hold our treasures in jars of clay and stand back and watch him work. Let us wait to be used by the Lord as he transforms us from glory to glory. Isaiah 6:8 says, "O Lord, you are our Father, we are the clay, and you are the potter; And all of us are the work of Your hand."

Giving our time, talent, and treasures to God sometimes is not on our radar. We cannot see how we can make room for it. We are overwhelmed with work, our families, busyness, things, etcetera, etcetera, etcetera. Many of us see lack rather than abundance. Surrender it all to God and watch him work.

Sometimes we get it twisted. So, let us untwist it. When we surrender all and focus on him, the care we give to God's time, talent, and treasure will be richly, outrageously, stupendously, and tremendously blessed. The Bible says that the blessings of God will overtake us (Deuteronomy 28:2) if we obey the voice of the Lord. "Eye hath not seen, nor ear heard," (1 Corinthians 2:9).

Prayer

Lord, I am ready to surrender all the cares and distractions that fill my life. I am ready to focus on you and to allow you to work in my life. Amen.

Reflection

What are my key takeaways from this teaching?

What adjustments do I need to make to have more time for God?

How can I enhance the way I use my gifts and talents?

What are my next steps?

Plop, Plop, Fizz, Fizz

Recently I had a devastating experience, one I venture to say that many others have. Oh, Lord, was my first cry. With adrenaline pumping, I went into rescue mode. The first-aid directions readily flooded my mind. I ran into the kitchen to gather supplies. Once I had done my best to triage the situation, I sat down and prayed. Truth be known, I wanted to start crying. Plop, plop, fizz, fizz—my phone fell into the toilet.

I spent several days without a phone, went to the repair shop, and finally bought a new one. I lost my pictures, my contacts, my text messages, and all my apps. But that is transitory stuff. What I missed the most was my Bible, devotionals, and scriptures. Those things have become such a part of my daily routine. That is kingdom-building stuff. The loss of my phone made me realize a couple of things.

First, I had not had my hands on my paper Bible since the last time I had pulled it out of its bag one Sunday at church. Now, that is a shame. I am kicking myself because I can do better. Some would say that is ok, read what you got. "Plop, plop, fizz, fizz." The Bible tells us in Psalm 119:11 to "hide the words in our hearts." Proverbs 22:18-19 tells us to "have them ready on our lips." Proverbs 7:3 says, "Bind them on your fingers; write them on the tablet of your heart." Deuteronomy 11:18 says, "Fix these words of mine in your hearts and minds; tie them as symbols on your hands and bind them on your foreheads." So, how can I "bind them to my fingers" or "tie them as symbols to my hands" if I do not touch my Bible? Amen. I have got to do something.

Secondly, I found that I am not as familiar with the Bible as I used to be. I once knew where the books were in the Bible as I knew where the letters were on my keyboard. I am sad to report that my electronic Bible has weakened my Bible dexterity. "Plop, plop, fizz, fizz." I have got to do better! I know the Bible. I have read the entire Bible, cover to cover, many times. When I touch my Bible, I turn the pages, interact with the text, write in it, highlight it, and talk with God. I cannot do that with my device. I am not advocating that anyone stop using their electronic Bible. I must touch the paper more often. "Plop, plop, fizz, fizz." God can use any situation, even a phone in the toilet, to get our attention and teach us a lesson. And through it all, we must do as Colossians 3:16 says, "Sing to God with gratitude in our hearts,"

Prayer

Heavenly Father, I love you and trust you. My earnest prayer is that I draw nearer to you through your word. Let your blessings and your glory fall afresh on me. Amen.

Reflection

What are my key takeaways from this teaching?

Do I include the word as a part of my daily routine?

How can I improve the quality of my Bible study?

What are my next steps?

Do you Believe?

My sister had a health challenge. Like most people, she was upset and fearful. She cried off and on for a month or so. I tried to console her by sitting with her, sharing my testimony, praying, and giving her encouraging scriptures.

I shared Psalm 30:5 with her. It says, "Weeping may endure for a night, but a shout of joy comes in the morning."

I shared Psalms 39:12 with her. It says, "Hear my prayer, O Lord, and listen to my cry; Do not be silent at my tears."

I shared Jeremiah 31:9 with her. It says, "They will come with weeping, and by prayer, I will lead them."

I would still find her crying. One day, I asked her, "Do you believe in Jesus?" She said yes. "Do you believe that he is the ultimate doctor?" She said yes.

"Do you believe that he healed the sick and raised the dead?" She said yes. "Do you believe that he is still in the miracle-making business?" She said, "Yes, Becky, I believe. Why do you keep asking me this?" I asked, "Then why are you still crying?"

Weeping is for a period, not forever. When we get ourselves into a state where we cannot do anything but cry day in and day out, it impacts our spiritual, mental, and physical health. Being a Christian does not mean we are perfect and will not cry, fear, or doubt. That is when we need our faith and belief in God the most. Remember, "everything is possible for one who believes," (Mark 9:23). Likewise, we may need to ask the Lord to help our unbelief (Mark 9:24). Romans 3:3 reminds our unbelief does not cancel God's faithfulness. He is faithful (Philippians 1:6). Thessalonians 5: 16-18 says we must be able to rejoice and be grateful for all things, especially during our time of test. On the other side of things is a great testimony. Amen!

Prayer

Lord, thank you for carrying me when I doubt, wiping my tears when I cry, and always loving me. I can do nothing without you. Great is your love and faithfulness. Amen.

Reflection

What are my key takeaways from this teaching?

About what do I need to stop crying?

I have 100% belief in the following:

What are my next steps?

Recap & Apply

How can I be a blessing to others?

How will I apply this learning to my life?

What do I need to do to receive a blessing?

How will I apply this learning to my life?

The B Word

When I was a young girl, each fourth Sunday was Missionary Sunday; the women were in charge. Sister Smith, one of the missionaries, would always lead the hymn *Everlasting Arms*. Her alto voice would sing, "What a fellowship, what a joy divine, leaning on the everlasting arms."

As a child, I did not understand the song. But as I got older and faced many hiccups, I understood that I could make it day by day, challenge by challenge, and trial by trial by leaning on the everlasting arms of God. I learned that I could triumph, be a victor, be an overcomer, and be truly blessed.

Oops, there is that word, the B word, blessed. The word bless is found 127 times in the King James Version of the Bible. Blessed is found 302 times and blessing 67 times. The Bible uses the word blessed in a different context than we do today. Blessed is used as a response to a greeting. "Hello. How are you doing?" The response may be one word, "Blessed." Popular culture has rolled blessed into the vernacular. For many, it is just something to say.

"I am too blessed to be stressed."

"I am blessed and highly favored."

"I am living a blessed life."

Much of what people are referencing as a blessing is about material gains. We reference physical, transitory, and things that do not matter in the grand scheme as we see in a mirror dimly. Back in the day, we knew we were blessed when we were "moving on up to the east side to a deluxe apartment in the sky. Finally got a piece of the pie." Or when we had a "diamond in the back, sunroof top." Or as my grandma would say, "We knew we were blessed when we had two nickels to rub together and one to keep in our pocket."

I am the first to admit that I like nice things. I consider myself blessed. Recently, I read a passage of scripture that I had read many times before; it gave me pause. One of the best definitions of the B word, blessed, is in the New Testament book of Matthew. In The Beatitudes (Matthew 5: 3-12), Jesus discussed being blessed.

3 Blessed are the poor in spirit: for theirs is the kingdom of heaven.

4 Blessed are they that mourn: for they shall be comforted.

5 Blessed are the meek: for they shall inherit the earth.

6 Blessed are they which do hunger and thirst after righteousness: for they shall be filled.

7 Blessed are the merciful: for they shall obtain mercy.

8 Blessed are the pure in heart: for they shall see God.

9 Blessed are the peacemakers: for they shall be called the children of God.

10 Blessed are they which are persecuted for righteousness sake: for theirs is the kingdom of heaven.

11 Blessed are ye, when men shall revile you, and persecute you, and shall say all manner of evil against you falsely, for my sake.

12 Rejoice, and be exceeding glad: for great is your reward in heaven: for so persecuted they the prophets which were before you.

There is that word again, blessed. Unlike many of us, Jesus was not referencing physical things, transitory things, or things that do not matter in the grand scheme. God is still in the blessing business and will give us material things. Psalm 37:4 says, "Delight yourself in the Lord, and he will give you the desires of your heart." Our world could use more peacemakers, more who are pure in heart, more who are merciful, and more who are meek. Let us remember, in all our getting, first get that blessed assurance in Christ Jesus.

Prayer

Lord, thank you for your many blessings. May you find in me some of the things spoken about in the Beatitudes. Your grace and your favor have prospered me in many ways. To whom much is given, much is required. Lead me as I endeavor to be a blessing to others. Amen.

Reflection

What are my key takeaways from this teaching?

The Lord has truly blessed me. I can list five of those blessings.

As I read the Beatitudes (Mathew 5: 3-12), which blessings do I need most?

What are my next steps?

Chosen: So Do Not Look Back

My previous workplace was home to scores of Sandhill cranes. These big brown birds are 3-5 feet tall and weigh 6-15 pounds. The first few times I saw them walking, I was afraid. One day, I was going back to my office after a meeting. It had rained. I was gingerly dodging the puddles that dotted the walkway. Out of the corner of my eye, I spotted four birds. They were coming my way. It looked like we were on an intersecting path. Determined that would not happen, I had two choices: speed up or slow down.

I decided to speed up. I began to power walk at a nice clip. Feeling good about my progression, I turned to look behind me to see how much distance I had put between me and the birds. Splat and splash! While looking back, the toe of my shoe hit an uneven crack in the sidewalk. I fell face down into a puddle. Ouch!

It was not a pretty sight. The birds indeed intersected my path. When they stepped past, I was so scared I could not holler. When I finally got up and got to my office—muddy, bloody, and wet—I asked myself, "Becky, why did you look back?"

At the first sign of danger, I called on the Lord for his strength and protection. I know God is always with me. I know this. He "is our refuge and strength, an ever-present help in a time of trouble," (Psalm 46:1). I know this, too. Hebrews 12:2 says he is "the author and finisher of the perfecter of our faith." I also know this; I have faith and believe in God and his power. But I cannot say why I looked back.

I am reminded of Lot's wife. Genesis 19:26 tells how she had safely escaped but looked back and turned into a pillar of salt. Abraham had pleaded with God on behalf of the people. Mercifully, God allowed Abraham's nephew, Lot, and his family to escape. These chosen few were told not to look back. Several commentaries discuss why Lot's wife turned around. Some say she turned to get a last look at what she was leaving; others say she turned to look for her daughter. No matter the reason, she was chosen and should not have looked back.

The word chosen means "one who is the object of choice or divine favor: an elect person." There are 276 instances of the word chosen in the Bible.

- Ephesians 1:4 says, "He chose us in Him before the foundation of the world."
- 2 Thessalonians 2:13 says, "God has chosen you from the beginning of salvation."
- John 15:16 says, "You did not choose me, but I chose you…"
- Matthew 22:14 says, "For many are called, but few are chosen."

God's chosen people should always keep their eyes on Jesus. Do not look to the left, look to the right, or look behind. The song says, "Keep your eyes and Jesus and you'll be just fine." Luke 9:62

says, "No one who puts his hand to the plow and looks back is fit for service." I read somewhere that God does not choose those who are fit, but outfits those whom he chooses." Lord, thank you for choosing and outfitting me.

Prayer

Father, I want to always be among your chosen. I remember Lot's wife. I will not turn back or look back. I will keep my eyes steady on you. My prayer is that I will be found worthy of your choice and fit for your service. Amen.

Reflection

What are my key takeaways from this teaching?

Have I ever looked back?

What distractions may take my focus off Jesus?

What are my next steps?

Upstaged

In October 1964, there was a historic concert in Santa Monica, California. There were three headliners: Chuck Berry, James Brown, and the Rolling Stones. Reportedly, Mick Jagger refused to leave his dressing room after James Brown's performance. It took Marvin Gaye to encourage him to go out and do his best. The Rolling Stones were supposed to close the event. However, they were upstaged by the Godfather of Soul.

I have a question. Who or what is upstaging the God of our soul? The God who is the alpha and the omega. The God who provides over and over and over again. The God who knew us before we were in our mother's womb. The God who gave his only begotten son. The Great I Am, the Rose of Sharon, El Shaddai, Jehovah Jireh, the Bright and Morning Star, the God of the second chance, and our comforter. Who or what is upstaging that God in our lives? Nothing should upstage God. We are individual members of the body of Christ. That is an awesome responsibility. To whom much is given, much is required.

Matthew 5:16 says, "Let your light shine before men, that they may see your good works, and glorify your Father which is in heaven." There are about 2.2 billion Christians. Sadly, there is so much darkness in our world. There is murder and mayhem, crimes against children and the elderly, theft, tech crimes, lawlessness in high places, wars, and rumors of wars. It sometimes feels like the world has turned its back on God. If the 2.2 billion of us were to all shine our lights, imagine how bright the world would be. Who or what is upstaging our God?

We are to carry out the Great Commission. Matthew 28:19 tells us, "Go ye therefore, and make disciples of all nations, baptizing them in the name of the Father, the Son, and the Holy Spirit." In our world, our country, our state, our city, our community, our family, our church, and our jobs, many are lost. Some are crying out for help. Do the 2.2 billion of us reach out and show the love of God? Or do we avert our eyes, hurriedly walk away, and leave the situation for someone else? Are we fishing, or do we need to cut bait? Who or what is upstaging our God?

There is so much work to do. Matthew 9:35 says, "The harvest is plentiful, but the laborers are few." Just imagine if 2.2 billion Christians, including you and I, used the time, talent, and resources God has entrusted us. What a difference we could make. Truth time, I need to do better. I have and do let things upstage God: my job, my family, my civic commitments, stress, drama, and downright foolishness. The busyness of my life sometimes crowds out quiet time and study time. Some days, I get up running, come home worn out, and fall into bed. Sometimes, I start to pray and then fall asleep mid-prayer. My light did not shine, and I did not fish. I let the transitory things of life upstage God.

I am not suggesting that any of this has happened to anybody else. I am being honest about my life and struggle to stop letting things upstage God. I use the word let, because I have a choice. If I am to be what the Bible says I am to be, I must stop letting and start choosing. Every time, not some of the time, but every time, I should choose the things of God. Amen.

Prayer

God, thank you for your mercy and grace. I know that even with my faults, you love me. Thou I struggle, I hold fast to your words in Lamination 3:22-23. Your steadfast love never ceases, your mercies never end, and great is your faithfulness. Amen.

Reflection

What are my key takeaways from this teaching?

Have I let anything upstage God?

Do I need to make different choices?

What are my next steps?

Nuggets of Encouragement: Receiving God's Blessing Through Our Christian Walk

What's Your Theme Song?

Each TV wrestler has a theme song. Some are more colorful than others. The song usually lets the opponent know what is in store for them. We are like wrestlers, except our battle is not against man. Ephesians 6:12 says, "For we wrestle not against flesh and blood, but against principalities, against powers, against the rulers of the darkness of this world, against spiritual wickedness in high [places]."

What is your theme song? How do we let the Enemy know, and how do we let those things that so easily beset us, the temptations of life, our worries, and our fears—how do we let those things know that they are in for trouble, trouble, trouble, trouble, trouble, that they do not want any and that we will not give in until we are victorious? How do you let them know? What is your theme song? Do we look at those things and sing, "Sometimes I feel like a motherless child," or "You did not create me to worry; you did not create me to fear."

Do you remember Epaphras? Colossians 4:12 says he was a servant of Christ Jesus, who was "always wrestling in prayer for you, that you may stand firm in all the will of God, mature and fully assured." Do we wrestle in prayer for others? Do we stand in the gap? Or do we always beg the Lord for our own needs? Do we sing, "It is me; it is me O Lord, standing in the need of prayer." Or do we sing, "I need thee, every hour I need thee." Or do we sing, "He's got the whole world in his hands." What is your theme song?

1 Timothy 4: 10 says, "Here is the motive of our toiling and wrestling because we have our hopes fixed on the ever-living God, who is the Savior of all mankind, and especially of believers." Do we believe that God is our refuge and strength, a very present help in trouble? Do we sing, "Come by here my Lord, come by here." Or do we sing, "Blessed be the name of the Lord." What is your theme song?

Do we know that the battle is not ours? 2 Chronicles 2: 15 says, "For the battle is not yours, but God's." Can we praise him? Can we acknowledge his awesomeness? Can we trust him for our provision, for our deliverance, for our finances, for our safety, for our healing? He's Jehovah Jireh (the Lord who provides), Jehovah Rapha (The Lord who heals us), Jehovah Nissi (the Lord our banner), and Jehovah Elohim (the Lord our God). Can we sing "Jesus, Jesus, Jesus, there is just something about that name." What is your theme song?

Prayer

Father, my theme song is one of victory. It tells how I got over, how you saved me, how you washed me, and how I became a new creature. Father, thank you for your loving kindness. Thank you for giving me a new song to sing. Amen.

Reflection

What are my key takeaways from this teaching?

Is my theme song appropriate to my current journey? Why/why not?

What would I include in a theme song for my loved ones?

What are my next steps?

Can We Talk

Recently, I overheard several students having a conversation. It was a lively conversation that engaged all of them. I was dumbfounded because I realized I had no idea what they were discussing; the topic of the conversation escaped my understanding. Speaking English, they used acronyms and spelled them out like LOL, OMG, ROTFL, IDK, and SMH. I walked away thinking I was so glad I did not need a special language to converse with God.

We can speak to God anytime, anywhere, any place, 365, 24/7. God is always available. He never takes a sick day; He is never on vacation. We never need an appointment. He never ignores us, kicks us to the curb, unfollows us, or unfriends us. He never stabs us in the back or scandalizes our name. He never gives us the side eye. He never feels some kind of way, he is never petty, and he never forsakes us.

I am so glad He does not have any of these human frailties, attitudes, or behaviors. We can tell God anything; there is no condemnation. We will not see it on social media or hear it from the lips of a friend who "is just saying and thinks you need to know." We can tell God our secrets. We can tell God our desires. We can tell God our fears.

Throughout the Bible, God spoke to many people. He spoke to Adam & Eve, Cain, Noah & his sons, Abraham & Sarah, Moses, Elijah, Samuel, Jeremiah, Paul, Aaron & Miriam, Isaac, Jacob, Sarah, Rebecca, Ezekiel, Job, David, Solomon, Isaiah, Jonah, Hosea, and Zechariah.

God is still speaking today. Sometimes, He speaks in a still small voice, through dreams, visions, situations, people, and miracles. God speaks to us in many ways, primarily through his word. So, how do we talk to God? We can do so through a prayer, a song, a praise, a shout. Speaking to God does not necessarily have to be out loud. God reads minds. Romans 8:27 says, "God already knows our deepest thoughts."

In our time of trouble, we will never get an "I'll call you back" text from God. 1 Corinthians 10:13 says he will never give us more than we can bear. He will provide a way out for us. Now, he may not come when we want him, but believe me, He is always right on time. He comes with what we need, many times with more than we can imagine. What an amazing God!

He is our ride-or-die. He is our creator (Genesis 1:1), our anchor (Hebrews 6:19), our strong tower (Proverbs 18:10), our comforter (2 Corinthians 1: 3-4), our dwelling place (Psalm 91:9), our rock (Psalm 18:2), our shepherd (Psalm 23:1), our healer (Jeremiah 17:14), our banner (Exodus 17:15), our provider (Psalms 34), our living water (John 7:38), our redeemer (Proverbs 19:25), our bread of life (John 6:35), and our way maker (Isaiah 43:15-16).

We are His sheep and know His voice. Let us make it our business to talk to God daily. There is no need to wait until He knocks on our door. We can always talk.

Prayer

God, I am so glad I can talk with you anytime. You are always there for me. You hear my cries and meet my needs. I pray never to be separated from you. Amen.

Reflection

What are my key takeaways from this teaching?

How do I talk to God?

What current situation do I need to talk to God about?

What are my next steps?

High Expectations

When my grandson was about three, my daughter called me one evening. Frustrated, she started the conversation with, "I want you to hear something. Your grandson has been going on like this for 45 minutes." I could hear him wailing in the background.

"What's wrong with him," I asked.

"I don't know, she said.

"Put him on the phone and let me talk to him."

"Kevin, what's the matter?"

"Daddy washed me," he said.

"He washed you?"

"Yeah, He put me in the shower, squirted some soap on the rag, rubbed it on my head, my face, my tummy, my feet, and my whole body. Then he turned the water on, it went all over me, and then put a big towel on me."

"Oh," I said. "Daddy gave you a bath."

Grandma, he didn't do like you do. Daddy didn't put me in the bathtub, no bubbles, no toys, and no music. I didn't like it Grandma; that's a no-no!"

Clearly what he expected bath time to be disagreed with what his father thought bath time should be.

This can happen to us. Expectations and reality are often not the same. What we expect or plan may not always be what God has planned. God has high expectations! Ask Mary, Esther, Isaac, Moses, Job, or Paul. Proverbs 16:9 says, "In their hearts, humans plan their course, but the LORD establishes their steps." An old Yiddish proverb says "We Plan – God Laughs." We are foolish to think that we are in control of anything, especially the tasks that God has assigned us. I am a planner. I like to dot my I's and cross my T's, twice. I have a Plan A, a Plan B, and a Plan C for every situation. I am not too fond of last-minute, messy things. But you know, this is an exercise in futility; it is all folly.

Matthew 6:30-33 assures us that we need not worry for God is in control. I like how the Message Bible put it, "If God gives such attention to the appearance of wildflowers—most of which are never even seen—don't you think he will attend to you, take pride in you, do his best for you? What I am trying to do here is to get you to relax, and not be so preoccupied with getting, so you can respond to God's giving. People who do not know God and the way he works fuss over these things, but you know both God and how he works. Steep your life in God-reality, God-initiative, God-provisions. Do not worry about missing out. You will find all your everyday human concerns will be met." Because we need not worry, it does not mean we should be slackers. God expects us to work.

God-ordained work. In Genesis 1:1-31 God worked. He created the earth and all things in it;

In Genesis 2:15, Adam was predestined to work. The Bible says, "God took the Man and set him down in the Garden of Eden to work the ground and keep it in order;"

In Exodus 20: 9, the fourth commandment tells us to work six days and rest on the seventh.

Colossians 3:23-25 tells us we are expected to do our best work, and not just do the minimum;

1 Thessalonians 4:11-12 reminds us to work with respect and honor and warns us about slothfulness; and

Ecclesiastes 5: 19 says, "We should make the most of what God gives, both the bounty and the capacity to enjoy it, accepting what has given and delighting in the work. It is God's gift!"

Remember, stewardship is good work; it is God's work. After the apostles heard Jesus' teaching on stewardship, they had but one response, "Lord, Increase our faith!" It is God who works in us to fulfill his good purpose. As we continue our work as stewards, remember Proverbs 16:3. It says, "Commit your work to the LORD, and your plans will be established." Let us meet the Lord's high expectations!

Prayer

Lord, enable me to meet your high expectations. I am willing to submit myself to your leadership and excited about our journey together. Thank you for your guidance and love. Amen.

Reflection

What are my key takeaways from this teaching?

Am I meeting high expectations in the work I do for the Lord?

What area might I need to improve my performance?

What are my next steps?

Nuggets of Encouragement: Receiving God's Blessing Through Our Christian Walk

Blind, but Now I See

I have been having problems sleeping; I sleep better in total darkness. However, some annoying light sources have disturbed my peace. They include the frequent flicker of my cell phone, the constant digital display of my cable box, and the occasional bursts of light from my neighbors' floodlights. The doctor recommended that I wear a sleep mask. I found a heavy-duty, total black-out mask.

The first night was great; I slept well, better than I had in months. It was better than good. However, I woke up blind. Immediately, I started to talk to the Lord. "Oh, Lord, what is this? I went to bed sighted and woke up blind. How will I be able to take care of myself? How will I be able to take care of Momma? What do you have for me in this season? What am I supposed to learn or teach? I know all things are according to your will. Lord, I need your help. I need an extra portion of your favor and your grace."

I reached up to wipe away a tear that rolled down my cheek and touched the sleep mask. I could not do anything but laugh. I pulled it off, blind, but now I see! I have thought of my "blind" moment many times. I have asked if I see. Have I devoted my life to serving God? To which of the roles, tasks, jobs, or duties assigned to me have I blind eyes? I was convicted to open both eyes—widely—to see and to do better. Have any of you ever had any blind moments in your life?

Older women sometimes turn blind eyes to younger ones. Titus 2:3-5 says, "Likewise, teach the older women to be reverent in the way they live, not to be slanderers or addicted to much wine, but to teach what is good. Then they can urge the younger women to love their husbands and children, to be self-controlled and pure, to be busy at home, to be kind, and to be subject to their husbands so that no one will malign the word of God."

Older men sometimes turn blind eyes to younger ones. Titus 2: 1, 6-8 says, "Older men are to be sober-minded, dignified, self-controlled, sound in faith, love, and steadfastness... Likewise, urge the younger men to be self-controlled. Show yourself in all respects to be a model of good works, and in your teaching show integrity, dignity, and sound speech that cannot be condemned, so that an opponent may be put to shame, having nothing evil to say about us."

Let us open our eyes widely. There are generations behind us that need us. Let us stop talking about generations X, Y, and Z, and start doing something. They need our help, our guidance, our prayers, our modeling, our mentoring, our intersession, our support, our example, and our touch. They are our future. They need to know the word of God, how to hide it in their hearts, how to use it, and how to live a victorious Christian life. That is our assignment.

We sometimes turn blind eyes to our duty as stewards to give our time, talent, money, and resources in service to God. Proverbs 3:9-10, in part, says, "Honor the LORD with your wealth, with the first fruits of all your crops; then your barns will be filled to overflowing…" We know what we are supposed to do; enough said.

We sometimes turn blind eyes to our duty to the poor. We will not even make eye contact with homeless people on the side of the road. We say get a job or make a judgment that they are going to take our money and use it for ill. Psalm 41:1 says, "How blessed is he who considers the helpless; The LORD will deliver him in a day of trouble."

We sometimes turn blind eyes to… you fill in the blank. There is so much work for us to do in our church, community, and world. Let us ask God for his guidance, let us ask him to order our steps, and let us put our hands on the plow. If not us, who? We are kingdom people. I believe, declare, and decree the Lord will mightily bless our efforts.

Prayer

Heavenly Father, open my eyes so that I can see clearly. Help me to temper blindness by keeping my eyes focused on you. Amen.

Reflection

What are my key takeaways from this teaching?

Are there things to which I have turned a blind eye?

What do I need God's help with to see clearly?

What are my next steps?

Keep Your Mouth

I am cleaning out my storage room. There is stuff in there I have not seen for at least five years. I have had several family members offer to assist me. One of the kids—hoping to find some hidden treasure—asked if they found something good would they be allowed to keep it. I thought about what my momma would say and I said "Yes, keep it and keep your mouth."

Christ during his ministry often told folks to keep their mouth. In Matthew, a large crowd followed Jesus. He healed the ones who were ill among them and "He warned them not to tell others about him," (Matthew 12:15-16). Keep your mouth. In Mark, Peter, James, and John were returning with Jesus from the mountain where Jesus had been transfigured. "Jesus gave them orders not to tell anyone what they had seen," (Mark 9:7-10). Keep your mouth. In Luke, Jesus raises Jarius' daughter from the dead. "Her parents were astonished, but he [Jesus] ordered them not to tell anyone what had happened," (Luke 8:51-56). Keep your mouth.

There are several other examples of Jesus telling folks to keep their mouths. Jesus heals two blind men (Matthew 9:27-30). Jesus casts out demons (Mark 3:11-12). Jesus heals a leaper (Matthew 7:35-37). After each of these events, Jesus tells them not to say anything. Keep your mouth.

The Bible also tells us how to keep our mouths shut during our everyday Christian walk. Proverbs is full of words of wisdom. Here are a few.

- Proverbs 21:23 says, "Whoever keeps his mouth and his tongue, keeps himself out of trouble."
- Proverbs 13:3 says, "Whoever guards his mouth preserves his life, he who opens wide his lips come to ruin."
- Proverbs 29:11 says, "A fool gives full vent to his spirit, but a wise man quietly holds it back."
- Proverbs 10:19 says in part, "Whoever restrains his lips is prudent."

So, we are admonished to keep our mouths. I boldly confess sometimes I find it hard to keep my mouth closed. Proverbs 18:21 says, "The tongue has the power of life and death." Even though I know this to be true, sometimes my tongue wants to wag. Daily, I am learning how to do a better job of keeping my mouth. Being a Christian is about living my life as examples of the goodness and mercy of God, and letting others see Jesus in me. I cannot be all God wants me to be with loose lips. I must guard the what, when, how, and why of what I say.

Ecclesiastics 3:7 says, "There is a time to be silent and a time to speak" and Proverbs 17:29 says, "Even a fool who keeps silent is considered wise." I want to learn the time to be silent and to be considered wise. Keep your mouth.

Prayer

Father, help me to keep my mouth closed. Not all things are intended to be shared. I need your guidance and your support as I move forward. Thank you for loving me. Amen.

Reflection

What are my key takeaways from this teaching?

Am I good at keeping my mouth?

What challenges do I have in keeping silent?

What are my next steps?

Recap & Apply

How can I be a blessing to others?

How will I apply this learning to my life?

What do I need to do to receive a blessing?

How will I apply this learning to my life?

Nuggets of Encouragement: Receiving God's Blessing Through Our Christian Walk

Change my Name

Most people had a nickname growing up; some people still have them. My family has a Sweetie, Tender, Precious, Peaches, Pookie, Special, Goo Goo, Peewee, Poopie, Red, Baby, Twin, Scootie, Shortie, Pepper Man, Mookie, and a Ma Dear. What a crew! Names are important. Some of us are old enough to remember the TV show "Roots." When Kunta Kinte was named, his father raised him into the sky as a blessing. The same happened when Simba was named in the "The Lion King." Names are important.

When you read the book of Genesis chapters 10-11, they are full of begets: from Noah to Abraham. So on begat this one and so on begat that one. Many of the names have special meanings. Names are important. In the Bible, you will read about several people whom God changed their names. The Bible does not say, but I believe when God changed a name, it was to establish a new identity for a person and to set them on a new journey, a new destiny.

Abram's name changed to Abraham. Genesis 17:5 says, "No longer will you be called Abram; your name will be Abraham, for

I have made you a father of many nations." Names are important. Sarai's name changed to Sarah. Genesis 17:15 says, "God also said to Abraham, as for Sarai your wife, you are no longer to call her Sarai; her name will be Sarah." The name Sarai means quarrelsome, and Sarah means princess. Names are important.

In Acts 9:1–19, we read of Saul on his way to Damascus. He was carrying a letter from the high priest in Jerusalem that gave Saul the authority to arrest any followers of Christ. On the road, the Lord met Saul, changed his name to Paul, and commissioned him to take the gospel to the Gentiles. Saul means demanded or death, and Paul means little or humble. Names are important.

Genesis 32: 22-32, tells the story of Jacob's name change. Jacob wrestled all night with someone. I have read different interpretations about who the wrestler was: some say a man, some say an angel, and some say God. It was not TV wrestling; it was holy ghost wrestling. At daybreak, the wrestler told Jacob to let him go. But Jacob replied, "I will not let you go unless you bless me." The man asked his name. "Jacob," he answered. The man said, "Your name will no longer be Jacob, but Israel because you have struggled with God and with humans and have overcome." Jacob means to undermine, and Israel means to prevail with God. Names are important.

Think about the names that we call ourselves and the names others call us. You know the ones: broken, unworthy, ugly, sick, stupid, less than, poor/broke, never enough, slow, in the way, unlovable. There are more; you fill in the blank. We all have moments of self-doubt. We are human, and we walk in the flesh. But remember, death and life are in the power of the tongue. God sees us as we are and loves us just the same. Names are important.

Think about the names we want the Almighty God to call us now and at the trumpet's last sound. You know the ones: prayer warrior, mighty man or woman of God, good and faithful servant, child of God, blessed, forgiven, believer, beloved, friend, my sheep, worthy, favored. There are more; you fill in the blank. We can call those things that are not, as though they were (Romans 4:17). For as a man thinks in his heart, so is he (Proverbs 23:7). Names are important. We do not need to wrestle with the Lord to change our names. Behold, he stands at the door and knocks. Let him in.

Prayer

Father, thank you for calling me by name. Your mercy, grace, and love sustain me. When you knock, I will answer. Amen.

Reflection

What are my key takeaways from this teaching?

What names do I call myself? Why?

What is the most important name I want to hear God call me?

What are my next steps?

Nuggets of Encouragement: Receiving God's Blessing Through Our Christian Walk

Ought To

The other day I saw a sign on a church marque. It said this is an "Ought to Biography." I am sure I am not by myself with a list of things I ought to do. I ought to stay out of the stores. I ought to drink more water. I ought to take more steps. I ought to study more. I ought to drink less coffee. This is my ought to biography; what is on your list? While in the grand scheme of things these may seem small, they matter. The Bible says it is the little foxes that spoil the vines (Song of Solomon 2:15). These little foxes remind me of the broken window theory. It suggests that as soon as you notice a "broken window" (it could be a bad habit, a wrong decision, an error in judgement, etc.), you should fix it immediately. If not, that one could lead to another.

For many of us, our lives are filled with little foxes and broken windows that go unnoticed, unaddressed, and/or ignored. How can we be about our father's business if we do not have a handle on our own? Before we do a thing, we must declare a thing. Job 22:28 says, "thou shalt also decree a thing and it shall shine upon thee and the light shall shine upon thy ways." Declaring a thing means to speak it aloud, to make it known, or to put it out there. This is easier said than done. Ridding our lives of the little foxes and the broken windows is not for the faint at heart. It takes work, courage, and a firm, unwavering belief in God. He restores, redeems, renews, and revives. "Some trust in chariots and horses, but we trust in the name of the Lord our God," (Psalms 20:7). God's plan done God's way does not lack God's provision. He is the way, the truth, and the life (John 14:6).

As Christians, there are lots of things we ought to do. We ought to pray without ceasing (1 Thessalonians 5:17), study to show ourselves approved (2 Timothy 2:15), be good stewards (1 Timothy 6: 17-21), witness to others (Jeremiah 1: 7-9), and give thanks (1 Thessalonians 5:18). We ought to also proclaim the word of God (2 Timothy 4: 2-5), practice obedience (Deuteronomy 5:33), fear God and not man (Proverbs 19:23), and be ready for God to use (Isaiah 6:8). We ought to be about kingdom work. Matthew 13:44 tells the Parables of the Hidden Treasure and the Pearl. The verse says, "The kingdom of heaven is like treasure hidden in a field. When a man found it, he hid it again, and then in his joy went and sold all he had and bought that field." Matthew 9:37 tells us that, "the harvest is plentiful, but the laborers are few."

We have work to do. This life is short; too short to be caught unaware, unprepared, upset, and unhappy. "Better one handful with tranquility than two handfuls with toil and chasing the wind," (Ecclesiastes 4:6). I heard a guy say, "Get rid of the nonsense, so you can use your common sense, so your life can make sense." Sounds good. I am planning to remove the word ought from my vocabulary. Instead, I am going to use the phrase "will do" and frame it in the positive instead of the negative. This is my "will do" biography. I decree it, declare it, and I am sticking to it.

Prayer

Almighty God, there are so many things I ought to do. Guide my steps, focus my eyes, open my mind, and fix my heart so I will be ready to be used by you. Amen.

Reflection

What are my key takeaways from this teaching?

What is one thing I ought to do?

What do I need from God to do it?

What are my next steps?

Is God Your Co-pilot?

One day, my momma and I were taking a leisurely drive. Along the way, we got behind a slow-moving driver. Momma was not pleased. "Becky, blow the horn. I bet that is some old coot licking on an ice cream cone. Blow the horn." I assured my 90-year-old Momma that I was not in a hurry and did not need to blow the horn.

After a few minutes, Momma grew impatient. To my surprise, she leaned over and blew the horn. I said, "Momma if there is any horn blowing to do, the driver is supposed to do it." She looked at me, smiled, and said, "You were not going to do it. That is why I did. Becky, sometimes you need a co-pilot."

Years ago, there was a bumper sticker going around that said, "God is my co-pilot." Think about that for a minute. If God is the co-pilot, who is the pilot? In my case, that means I am the pilot. That is a frightening thought. Without the leading of the Lord, I would be in the ditch with the others led by the blind leaders referred to in Matthew 15: 14-16.

I need God's leading. I need him to be the pilot of my life. Without him, where would I be? Proverbs 3:5-6 tells us to trust in the Lord and lean not to our understanding. In Psalm 32:8 God assures us, "I will guide you along the best pathway for your life."

We all have a predestined path, one that God designed for us before we were in our mother's womb. Sometimes, in our ultimate wisdom, we allow our will to override the leading of God. We become the pilots of our lives. Proverbs 16:9 says, "We can make our plans, but the Lord determines our steps."

Proverbs 4:26 warns, "Give careful thought to the paths for your feet and be steadfast in all your ways." The keywords in this passage are careful and steadfast. The dictionary says careful means "making sure of avoiding potential danger, mishap, or harm; cautious." Steadfast means "resolutely, dutiful, firm, and unwavering"

In the Bible, several people were careful. Joseph & Mary were careful to obey God's directions about preparing for the birth of the Christ child. Moses was steadfast in following God's lead to rescue the Israelites. None of them needed a co-pilot, they needed the Almighty. Deuteronomy 31:8 says the Lord goes before us and prepares the way. He did it for Joseph, Mary, and Moses. He will do it for us. Romans 8:14 reminds us, "Those who are led by the spirit of God are sons of God."

I want to be led by God. I want him to be the pilot. I do not even want to be the co-pilot. The prefix "co" assumes we are equal in this thing. We are not. He is the potter; I am the clay. I am determined to remain steadfast, focused, fearless, and fierce. I will be careful to hear God's voice, not to lean to my understanding, and not to come to my conclusions or solutions. God does not need my help. I need his. I will occupy the passenger seat. He is the pilot; I have been blessed because of it.

Prayer

Lord, thank you for being my pilot. Thank you for leading me, allowing me to walk in your footprints, and carrying me on occasion. I am lost without you. Amen.

Reflection

What are my key takeaways from this teaching?

Is God my co-pilot or my pilot?

What changes do I need to make as I navigate this life?

What are my next steps?

Do You Hear Him?

I believe God still speaks to people. There are 680 references in the Bible about the voice of God. The Bible says in Matthew 11:15, "Whoever has ears, let him hear." Do we hear the Lord? We might, sometimes, half of the time, always, never; you choose. Sometimes God's voice is loud and clear, sometimes a whisper, and sometimes we hear it in bits and pieces because we have a bad connection.

Several people of old heard God's voice.

- In Genesis 3:8, we read about Adam; he heard God in the "cool of the evening."
- In Deuteronomy 4:12, we read about Moses; he heard God in the "midst of the fire."
- In 1 King 19: 12-13, we read about Elijah; he heard the Lord as a "still small voice." And,
- In Job 38:1, we read about Job; he heard the Lord out of a whirlwind.

God was telling them something!

I have had lots of challenges. Throughout them all, I believe God was talking. He was trying to tell me something. One year, things were overwhelming for me and members of my family. There was a cancer prognosis, surgeries, and chemotherapy. I was a caregiver of sorts to all.

I worked 12-14 hours, 2-3 days a week. My computer crashed, I lost 12 years of data, and the lawn mower ate my keys. Additionally, we had a leak at my house that revealed black mold and asbestos. We had to move out of the house.

Boy, was God trying to tell me something! My momma would say the Lord was speaking "mighty loud." Sadly, I was like Samuel. The Bible says in 1 Samuel 3:7 that the Lord spoke to Samuel, but he did not recognize the Lord's voice. God consistently speaks to us. Many times, we do not hear him. His voice is often muffled by the clutter and chatter of life.

The Lord did not speak to me in the cool of the evening, through a burning bush or a whirlwind, or in a still small voice. He spoke to me through sickness, a dead computer, a fist full of mangled keys, and a broken toilet. I did not initially hear him because I was trying to take things into my own hands, shoulder responsibilities, and make decisions I should have left to him.

What was he saying, you ask? "I got this… I will not put more on you than you can bear (1 Corinthians 10:13). I will give you rest (Matthew 11:28). I am an ever-present help in a time of trouble (Psalm 46:1). I will send you a comforter (John 15:26). Lean not to your own understanding (Proverbs 3:5). be anxious for nothing (Philippians 4:6). All things work together for the good (Romans 8:28). My grace is sufficient for thee (2 Corinthians 12:9). If I am for you, who can be against you (Romans 8:31). I got this. My Lord, what a promise! Amen and Amen.

I believe God still speaks to people. Do we understand what he is saying? Proverbs 2:2-6 says, "turning your ear to wisdom and applying your heart to understanding—indeed, if you call out for insight and cry aloud for understanding, and if you look for it as for silver and search for it as for hidden treasure, then you will understand the fear of the Lord and find the knowledge of God. For the Lord gives wisdom; from his mouth come knowledge and understanding." Let us "Seek him while he may be found; call on him while he is near" (Isaiah 55:6). Wisdom, understanding, and knowledge will help us to hear God's voice more clearly.

Prayer

God, help me to hear your voice. Are you trying to tell me something? Is it something about how I am living, my stewardship, my beliefs, my decisions, or my actions? Lead me in my quest to seek wisdom, understanding, and knowledge. Amen.

Reflection

What are my key takeaways from this teaching?

Do I hear God speaking to me?

About what do I need to talk to God?

What are my next steps?

S.A.V.I.O.R.

Jesus is the reason for the season. We hear this so much during December that it is almost trite. Most of us know the story of the birth, crucifixion, and resurrection of Jesus. We mark these events: Christmas and Easter. Along with Mother's Day, they are among the most attended church days of the year.

What about Jesus on the other 362 days? He should be the reason for every day, not just Christmas and Easter. Galatians 6:9 says in due season you will reap. It did not say on Christmas you will reap. It did not say on Easter you will reap. It says in due season you will reap. If we believe this, Jesus must be S.A.V.I.O.R. in our lives.

S is for strength. To do anything, great or small, we need to have strength. The dictionary says strength is the quality or state of being strong: physical power and energy or emotional or mental qualities necessary for dealing with situations or events that are distressing or difficult. As we journey through this season, we need every ounce of strength. The adversary is suited up and lying in wait. We need to remember to call on Jesus. Isaiah 40:29 says, "He's the one who gives might to the faint, renewing strength for the powerless." Philippians 4:13 says, "I can do all things through Christ who strengthens me." S is for strength.

A is for anchor. An anchor keeps something in place; it is a reliable mainstay. That describes God's love for us. He is unchangeable, and he cannot lie. Our hope in him is "firm and secure like an anchor for our souls," (Hebrews 6:19). The ebbs and flows of this life may toss us about or move us off course. Jesus can keep us steadfast. A is for anchor.

V is for Victor. A victor is a person who defeats an enemy or opponent in a battle, game, or other competition. In battle, to be victorious, we need to be like Superman. He always has on his suit and can tear it away at notice. He is invincible in that suit. We must put on our war clothes, the full armor of God (Ephesians 6: 11-17). We are invincible in that suit. The hand of God strengthens and helps us (Isaiah 41:10). Proverbs 21:31 says, "Victory belongs to the Lord." V is for Victor.

I is for intercessor. An intercessor is a person who intervenes on behalf of another, especially by prayer. Jesus is the ultimate intercessor. We are his people (Isaiah 51:16). He intercedes for us when we lose our way and fall into sin. I am an imperfect person; my prayers alone are not enough. I am glad and grateful that the Lord, Jesus Christ, intercedes on my behalf. Be assured, God has us engraved on the palm of his hand (Isaiah 49:16). Like Peter, I revere Christ as Lord and am prepared to tell everyone about my hope in Jesus (1 Peter 3:15). I is for intercessor.

O is for one and only. The first commandment says, "You shall have no other gods before Me." Isaiah 46:9 says, "Remember the former things of old: for I *am* God, and *there is* none else; *I am* God, and *there is* none like me." He is God all by himself! The alpha and the omega, the I am, the bright and morning star, the wheel in the middle of the wheel, the rose of Sharon, our refuge and strength, a very present help in a time of trouble, and our comforter. O is for one and only.

R is for redeemer. The words redeemer, redeem, and redemption appear 149 times in the Old Testament and 18 in the New Testament. The Bible identifies the redeemer. "As for our redeemer, the Lord of hosts is his name, the Holy One of Israel," (Isaiah 47:4). The Bible also asks for the redeemer's provision. Psalm 44:26 says, "Rise, be our help, and redeem us for the sake of your lovingkindness." Finally, the Bible acknowledges the redeemer's gifts. "It is because of him that you are in Christ Jesus, who has become for us wisdom from God—that is, our righteousness, holiness, and redemption," (1 Corinthians 1:30). Jesus is our blessed redeemer. Job 19:25 should be our battle cry. It says, "I know that my redeemer lives and that in the end, he will stand on the earth." R is for redeemer.

Let us be sure to have a S.A.V.I.O.R. — strength, an anchor, a victor, an intercessor, a one and only, and a redeemer in our lives. Jesus is always the reason.

Prayer

Jesus, our blessed redeemer, thank you for being our S.A.V.I.O.R. We are blessed because of your sacrifice, blood, and love for us. Amen.

Reflection

What are my key takeaways from this teaching?

S.A.V.I.O.R. — Which letter has the most significance to me?

S.A.V.I.O.R. — Which letter do I need to reintroduce to myself?

What are my next steps?

Work to Do

I recently heard an IT guy say 99% right is 100% wrong. I recalled a song my dad used to sing, "99 ½ Won't Do." The song says, "Lord, I'm trying, trying to make 100, 99 ½ won't do." I am an old chick and sometimes I am baffled by how some people do things. And, that may be because I am an old chick.

What baffles me is that some folks do ok, mediocre, will do, shabby, raggedy, halfway, fair to middling, so-so, second-rate, passable, poor, humdrum, thrown together, or plain sorry work, and have the audacity to think it is alright.

As a kid, my parents had two mantras that I still live by. My dad used to say to be the best at what you do and do it as if your signature is on it. My mom would say leave things better than you found them or do not put your hands on them. The Bible says in Colossians 3:23, "Whatever you do, work at it with all of your heart, as working for the Lord, not for human masters."

Work has been around since the beginning of time. The first work recorded in the Bible is God's creation work. For six days he labored; on the seventh day, he rested. If it was good enough for God, what about the rest of us? God's command for us to work began with Adam in the Garden of Eden (Genesis 2:15).

The words toil or work can be found in the Bible 480 times. From that, we can conclude that God thought work was an important part of our lives. There are many reassuring scriptures about work.

- Proverbs 16:3— "Commit to the Lord whatever you do, and he will establish your plans."
- Psalm 90:17— "May the favor of the Lord our God rest on us; establish the work of our hands for us—yes, establish the work of our hands."
- Ecclesiastes 3:22— "So I saw that there is nothing better for a person than to enjoy their work because that is their lot. For who can bring them to see what will happen after them?"
- Ecclesiastes 5:19— "Moreover, when God gives someone wealth and possessions, and the ability to enjoy them, to accept their lot and be happy in their toil—this is a gift of God."

Frances Crosby's song says, "To the Work! To the Work! We are servants of God; Let us follow the path that our Master has trod; With the balm of His counsel our strength to renew; Let us do with our might what our hands find to do."

Through work, we can fulfill the Great Commission (Matthew 28: 16-20) to spread the word of God. People watch us, our actions, our body language, and they hear our words. Through us, others may be drawn towards or turned away from God. Kingdom building is hard, yet rewarding work.

The Apostle Paul in 1 Corinthians 15:58 gave encouragement that still applies today. "Therefore, my dear brothers and sisters, stand firm. Let nothing move you. Always give yourselves fully to the work of the Lord, because you know that your labor in the Lord is not in vain." Matthew notes that the harvest is plentiful, but the workers are few (Matthew 9: 35-38).

Our work can sometimes be challenging. We do not like work, we do not like the people, we are not appreciated, we are overworked, we are mistreated, we are underpaid, and so on. We all have a story. Regardless of the situation, my God can make everything work together for our good. Remember, the dictionary is the only place where success comes before work. The work is plentiful, the victory depends on how we show up and what we do.

Prayer

Father, no matter what, I want to do my work as to the Master and I be found a good and faithful servant. I am a willing worker and pray for your grace to see me through. Amen.

Reflection

What are my key takeaways from this teaching?

What do I find satisfying about my work?

What aspects of my work habits can I improve?

What are my next steps?

Close Enough for a Blessing

Near the end of each year, people reflect on the resolutions, declarations, decrees, goals, and promises they made to themselves. It is also time to review the accomplishments, failures, and how close one came to success.

Motivation gets one started; habit keeps one going. Nonetheless, there is something about being close. Some say close only counts in hand grenades and horseshoes. I beg to differ; being close to the Lord is an incredible blessing.

Just ask the woman with the issue of blood. You might remember her story in the gospels of Matthew, Mark, and Luke. Luke 8:44 says the woman "came behind him, [speaking of Jesus], and touched the border of his garment; and immediately her issue of blood staunched." She was close enough to receive a blessing.

Close sometimes gets the prize. Ask the man who had been an invalid for 38 years. Annually, the Pool of Bethesda stirred. The first in was healed of his afflictions. When Jesus saw the man, he asked, "Do you want to get well?" The man said, "I have no one to help me into the pool when the water is stirred. While I am on my way, someone else goes in before me." Jesus told him, "Get up, pick up your mat, and walk." The man was immediately made well and he walked, (John 5: 5-9). He was close enough for a blessing.

John 9:6-7 talks about a man who was blind from birth. Jesus spat on the ground, made mud from the saliva, put it on the man's eyes, and told him to go and wash in the Pool of Siloam. The man did as he was told. The Bible says in verse 7, "He went home seeing." He was close enough for a blessing.

Remember Zacchaeus? Luke 19: 1-7 talks about the wealthy tax collector who desired to see Jesus. Because he was short, he climbed into a sycamore tree to see Jesus as he passed. Verse 6 says, "And when Jesus came to the place, he looked up and saw him, and said unto him, Zacchaeus, make haste, and come down; for today I must abide at thy house." Zacchaeus was close enough for a blessing.

God is still in the blessing business. Are we positioned to receive them? What did we do in the past to put God first in our lives? What more can we do in the present? What did we do in the past to spread the gospel, to be fishers of men as commanded by the Great Commission? What more can we do in the present? What did we do in the past with our time, talent, money, and resources? What more can we do in the present? In the past, were we close enough to God for a blessing? What more can we do in the present? Once we review what we did and think about what we can do, let us propose what we will do.

If we commit our resolutions, declarations, decrees, goals, and promises to God, we will be close enough to receive a blessing. James 4:8 says, if we draw near to God, he will draw near to us.

Prayer

Heavenly Father, I thank you for bringing me close to you. I may not always stay on the path, but you allow me to stumble and offer your extended hand to lift me. Your grace is sufficient for me. Amen

Reflection

What are my key takeaways from this teaching?

Am I close enough for a blessing?

What do I need to do to move closer to God?

What are my next steps?

What are you Waiting For?

Why wait? Have you ever said, "I'll do so and so when such and such happens"? Or have you said, "I'll do so and so, tomorrow?" I have. My dad used to say, "Today is the tomorrow that you talked about yesterday." So, my question is, what are you waiting for? Many of us spend our lives wanting and waiting. Are we waiting in the right way for the right thing? What are we waiting for?

We are waiting for our ship to sail in. We are waiting for the perfect mate. We are waiting for our children to act right. We are waiting for things to happen on our job. We are waiting for... You fill in the blank. But, are we waiting in the right way for the right thing? What are we waiting for?

Psalm 27:14 tells us to, "Wait for the Lord; be strong and take heart and wait for the Lord." That my friends, is more than a notion. We live in a fast-paced world. We can send news around the globe in the blink of an eye. We drive fast, we talk fast, we eat fast. The idea that we must wait sometimes rocks our world. We wait in line; we hate it. We wait in traffic; we hate it. We hate waiting for service, for the doctor, for the hairdresser, the barber, or our meal at a fast-food place. We hate it.

The word wait means, to remain or rest in expectation; to stay in one place until another catches up; to remain or be in readiness; or to remain temporarily neglected, unattended to, or postponed. The word wait appears 106 times in 101 verses in the King James Version of the Bible. The word waited appears 35 times, waiteth appears 11 times and waiting appears 8 times. Waiting must be important.

In Psalm 40:1 David said, "I waited patiently for the LORD; he turned to me and heard my cry." Isaiah 64:4 says, "Since ancient times no one has heard, no ear has perceived, no eye has seen any God besides you, who acts on behalf of those who wait for him."

So now my question is, are we waiting in the right way for the right thing? How can we wait for the Lord if we hate waiting and spend our time waiting in the wrong way for the wrong things? Patience is the key to waiting and waiting in the right way for the right thing. Romans 8:25 reminds us, "If we hope for what we do not yet have, we wait for it patiently."

The Bible says "I will wait for the God of my salvation (Micah 7:7). Our soul waits for the Lord; he is our help and our shield (Psalm 33:20). The Lord waits to be gracious to you (Isaiah 30:18). He is good to those who wait for him (Lamentations 3:25). he is not slow to fulfill his promise, but is patient toward you (2 Peter 3:9). I wait for the Lord, my soul waits (Psalm 130:5).

We must ask ourselves, what are we waiting for? What hinders us from using our time, talent, money, and resources for the kingdom? What are we waiting for? God is always at work. In ways seen and unseen, he is on the JOB, working things out for our good. He allows us to "call those things which be not as though they were." If we trust in him and wait on him, nothing will keep us from becoming the stewards he has called us to be. Amen.

Isaiah 40:31 says, "But those who hope in the Lord will renew their strength. They will soar on wings like eagles; they will run and not grow weary; they will walk and not be faint." What are you waiting for?

Prayer

Lord, thank you for your patience and your loving kindness. There are things I need to do and I need your guidance as I wait. I trust you and know you are working for my good. Amen.

Reflection

What are my key takeaways from this teaching?

What am I waiting for?

What do I need to do to move from waiting to doing?

What are my next steps?

Nuggets of Encouragement: Receiving God's Blessing Through Our Christian Walk

Recap & Apply

How can I be a blessing to others?

How will I apply this learning to my life?

What do I need to do to receive a blessing?

How will I apply this learning to my life?

About the Author

A church liturgist, Sunday School and Vacation Bible School teacher, and Bible study instructor are a few of the roles Dr. Rebekah McCloud has held. In 2004, she added church historian to the list when awarded the Rhea Marsh and Dorothy Smith Winter Park History Research Grant sponsored by the Winter Park Public Library and Rollins College. Her project and resulting book, Across the Tracks: A Collective History of Black Churches of Winter Park (FL), chronicles the history of the six oldest Black churches in Winter Park. Her follow-up to the project, sponsored by the City of Winter Park, was a book, Sacred Places, Sacred History: Black Churches of Winter Park. It chronicled the beginnings of Winter Park and Hannibal Square, the development of the twelve churches, and several of the citizens who contributed to the development of the West Side. She has continued that work over the years by photographing and collecting information on more than 50 historic black churches in Florida, Georgia, and Alabama. Currently, Dr. McCloud is working on a series of Christian journals. A retired educator who most recently served as the Executive Director of TRIO Programs at the University of Central Florida

(UCF), Dr. McCloud is a former school principal and an awarded classroom teacher who has taught undergraduate and graduate courses at several institutions. An author and award-winning journalist, she served on the editorial review board for six national peer-reviewed journals. She has shared her wisdom through over 200 workshops at local, state, regional, and national conferences. A versatile educator, in addition to being a certified Florida teacher and school administrator, she is a Certified Life Coach, a Certified Practitioner in Financial Capability, and a certified Financial Education Instructor. Dr. McCloud holds an Ed.D. in Curriculum & Instruction, a M.S in Business (Managerial Leadership), a M.Ed. in Education (Educational Leadership), a B.A. in Communications, and a Graduate Certificate in Career & Technical Education.

Further Study

For Further Study, see the three journals in the series:
- Journal 1— Nuggets of Encouragement: Living Each Day with Grace & Love
- Journal 2— Nuggets of Encouragement: Receiving God's Blessing Through Our Christian Walk
- Journal 3—Nuggets of Encouragement: Learning to Trust and Have Faith in God

Praise for *Nuggets of Encouragement*
What Readers Are Saying

Nuggets of Encouragement is a devotional that points the reader straight to the word of God. Each nugget contains personal stories and anecdotes that connect everyday life to scripture. I am personally enriched by the verses that are carefully selected in each writing. This devotional is an excellent resource for both personal reflection and group study. You will be blessed to grow and learn from the biblical applications in each nugget!
—Hiroko Vargas

Dr. Rebekah's Nuggets of Encouragement is full of wisdom and insight! This transformative book is your roadmap to life and life choices, dedicated to providing valuable guidance, inspiration, and practical advice to viewers. By serving as a guidepost, Nuggets of Encouragement offers readers a roadmap to navigate life's challenges and make informed decisions. The thought-provoking content sparks introspection, encourages personal growth, and empowers individuals to make conscious choices that align with their values and aspirations. Dr. McCloud provides engaging segments that present a collection of powerful insights and lessons from various sources, including ancient wisdom, spiritual teachings, philosophical concepts, and personal experiences. Whether you are seeking clarity, motivation, or a deeper understanding of yourself and the world around you, this book offers a treasure trove of wisdom to enrich and elevate your life journey. Explore the depths of wisdom and insight to help you on your path to personal growth and fulfillment.

—Dr. Tuyna Griffin, Founder & CEO, Black Women's Voices

Gifted, called, and anointed for a time such as this, Dr. Rebekah McCloud is walking in her divine calling. She is doing what she does best. I have enjoyed reading Dr. Rebekah McCloud's nuggets. She is very knowledgeable of the word of God and she always incorporates her life experiences into her nuggets. So glad to see her walking in her calling. She is a very kind person and she represents the Father well. I look forward to hearing future words of wisdom from Dr. Rebekah. Keep those nuggets coming!

—Patricia Eason, CEO, Angels Without Wings

Thank you, Dr. Rebekah, for this thought-provoking, inspirational, encouraging, and uplifting journal of daily nuggets to help get you through the day and beyond. I love your candid personal stories and how refreshing you have a way with words. I pray that this journal will bless all who read it. May God bless you and keep you always and that you remain in the center of His will.

—Patricia Washington, Pastor, Grace for Living Ministries

I do not believe anyone is more excited about this journal than I am. I have been the recipient of Dr. McCloud's wisdom, spirituality, humor, and amazing storytelling since 2019. Dr. McCloud's devotions have encouraged, inspired, and challenged me in my daily walk with Christ. I have been asking her for years to put her weekly nuggets into a book. I plan to be the first to order this journal, and I pray that if you are reading this you will join me in supporting this phenomenal woman and the gift that God has placed inside of her.

—Dr. Coretta Cotton

www.ingramcontent.com/pod-product-compliance
Lightning Source LLC
Chambersburg PA
CBHW031421290426
44110CB00011B/472